Jennifer Capriati

PHOTO CREDITS
Allsport: cover, pg. 2, 10, 13, 18 and 29
Wide World: pg. 6, 9, 14, 17, 21, 22, 25, 26 and 30

Distributed to Schools and Libraries
in the United States by
ENCYCLOPAEDIA BRITANNICA EDUCATIONAL CORP.
310 S. Michigan Avenue
Chicago, Illinois 60604

Library of Congress Cataloging-in-Publication Data
Rothaus, James.
Jennifer Capriati / Jim Rothaus.
p. cm.
Summary: A biography of the exciting tennis player who,
in 1990, became the youngest player ever to reach the final
in a women's tennis tournament.
ISBN 0-89565-738-4
1. Capriati, Jennifer—Juvenile literature.
2. Tennis players—United States—Biography—Juvenile literature.
[1. Capriati, Jennifer. 2. Tennis players.] I. Title.
GV994.C36R68 1991   91-17849
796.342′092—dc20   CIP
[B]   AC

Jennifer Capriati

by James R. Rothaus

The Virginia Slims of Florida usually isn't a big women's tennis tournament. There isn't a lot of money to be won. It isn't as important as Wimbledon, the U.S. Open, or even the French Open. But the 1990 Virginia Slims of Florida was a special tournament. Newspaper and television reporters came from all over the country. They came to see the future of women's tennis. They came to see thirteen-year-old Jennifer Capriati.

The tournament was Capriati's first as a pro. She was still a couple of weeks away from turning fourteen. The experts were saying Capriati would become one of the top ten women's players in the world before she was old enough to drive. "She's just a happy-go-lucky kid," said Rick Macci, who used to coach Capriati. "But put a tennis racket in her hand and . . . " Macci then shook his head. "I'm telling you. She's scary."

When the tournament began, Capriati seemed nervous. She didn't play well in her first couple of matches, but she still won them. Capriati then got better and better. She made the championship match, becoming the youngest player ever to reach the final in a women's tennis tournament. In the final, Capriati lost to Gabriela Sabatini, the third best player in the world. "I had to play my best tennis to beat her," Sabatini said after the match. "She should be at the top very soon."

The legend of Jennifer Capriati was born. Billie Jean King, one of the greatest women's players ever, was already a fan of Jennifer's. "It's really fun for me to see somebody her age and how well she handles things," said King, who played doubles with Capriati in the tournament. "Jennifer's certainly exciting to watch," stated Tracy Austin, another former great player. "Players like her come along once a decade."

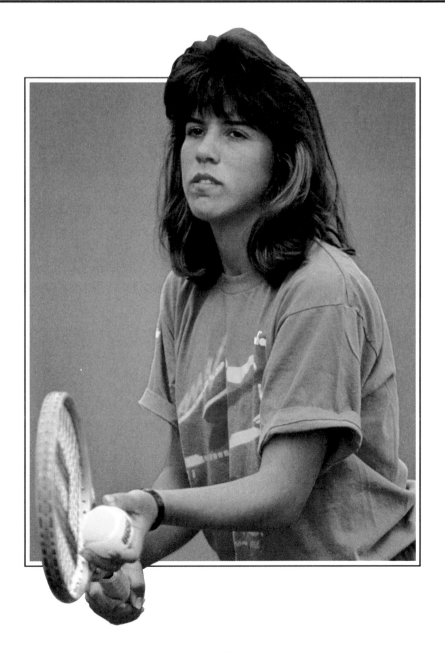

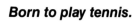

Jennifer Capriati was born March 29, 1976. Her father, Stefano, was a former soccer player who later took up tennis. Her mother, Denise, was also a good athlete. Before Jennifer was born, Stefano Capriati had taught Denise how to play tennis. He wanted his children to play tennis, too. "Stefano knew she [Jennifer] would be a tennis player before she was even born," Denise recalled.

Stefano had Jennifer do
sit-ups when she was an infant.
"She was a strong baby," her father
remembered. "She liked to crawl
behind the [tennis] ball machine and
play with the balls when I taught
tennis." Jennifer first picked up a
tennis racket when she was three
years old. A year later Stefano
decided his daughter needed a
tennis coach. He took Jennifer to
see Jimmy Evert, a pro in Fort
Lauderdale, Florida.

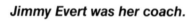 *Jimmy Evert was her coach.*

Jimmy Evert knew how to train young tennis players. His oldest daughter, Chris, became one of the greatest women's players of all time. When Jimmy Evert saw four-year-old Jennifer, he just shook his head. "She's too young for me," he said to Stefano. After all, Jimmy Evert hadn't started coaching Chris Evert until she was six. "Wait a minute," Stefano said. "First, see her play. I think she can hit the ball."

Stefano was right. Four-
year-old Jennifer could hit the ball
as well as most girls twice her age.
Jimmy Evert agreed to coach
Jennifer. The lessons lasted five
years. Jennifer even got to play
with her idol, Chris Evert. "The
first time I practiced with her,"
Jennifer recalled, "I was so nervous
I couldn't keep the ball in the court.
She probably thought I was <u>so</u> bad."

21

Steffi Graf and Jennifer.

But Chris Evert could tell how good Jennifer was going to be. Chris even gave the youngster a bracelet that said, "To Jennifer. Love Chris." To this day, Capriati never takes that bracelet off. She even tries to model her game after Evert's. But Jennifer is a more powerful player than Evert was. Capriati's serves are harder, and she plays better at the net.

When she was twelve years old, Capriati won two tournaments for girls eighteen years old and younger. She was beating girls five and six years older than she was. In 1988 Capriati became the youngest girl ever to win a youth national championship. A year later she won the juniors titles at both the French Open and the U.S. Open. She was too good for anybody but the pros, but she had to wait until a month before her fourteenth birthday to turn professional.

At the Virginia Slims of Florida tournament, Jimmy Evert sat in the stands and watched his former pupil. "It gives me a special feeling watching Jennifer do this," he said softly. Jimmy Evert had started Jennifer on the road to becoming a great player. It was now Stefano Capriati's job to guide her the rest of the way. Many tennis experts wondered if Jennifer would be pushed too hard, too fast. Other young stars such as Tracy Austin and Andrea Jaeger became burned out before they turned twenty.

"**A**s a parent," Stefano Capriati explained, "it is important to me that she enjoys her game. I want to see her smile and be happy." Stefano knows that he has to give Jennifer time to be a kid, time to get away from tennis. "She won't be out there playing in tournaments week after week after week," he said. Tracy Austin offered some tips for Jennifer. "She has to learn to take her time. If she gets hurt, she has to listen to what her body is telling her," Austin said.

It's important to enjoy the game.

"**T**he most important thing for her is to enjoy tennis, even when she starts losing," Austin explained. "She's got to develop her game and not worry about winning. If she can, then the sky's the limit." Jennifer doesn't worry about much of anything. Tennis is still fun for her, and it's most fun when people are yelling for her to do well. "When I hear the crowd getting into it," Capriati explained, "I really get into it too." That's when Jennifer Capriati becomes one of the best players in the game.